Original title:
Where the Light Falls

Copyright © 2025 Creative Arts Management OÜ
All rights reserved.

Author: Rory Fitzgerald
ISBN HARDBACK: 978-1-80581-768-0
ISBN PAPERBACK: 978-1-80581-295-1
ISBN EBOOK: 978-1-80581-768-0

## Serenity's Radiant Echo

In a world of giggles so bright,
Chasing shadows takes flight.
Butterflies slip on candy clouds,
As laughter forms whimsical crowds.

Socks mismatched in a dainty style,
Every glance brings a silly smile.
Sunbeams tickle the sleepy trees,
A dance of joy in the summer breeze.

## The Dance of Warm Embraces

In pajamas made for a daring spree,
We twirl in dreams by the old oak tree.
The sun's a jokester, throwing rays,
While we sneak snacks in a daze.

Silly shadows waltz on the wall,
We stumble and giggle, oh what a fall!
Each hug a bounce filled with sweet cheer,
Life's a circus, let's volunteer!

## Gleams of Yesterday's Memories

Polka dots marching on picnic sheets,
Chocolate stains from our wild treats.
Silly songs from the depths of our hearts,
Memories echo like clumsy dart arts.

Fuzzy socks and a pirate's hat,
Imaginary quests, can you handle that?
As sunshine giggles through dusty old glass,
We toast to the moments that surely won't pass.

## The Shimmering Promise

A wink from a cloud, a promise bestowed,
As mismatched shoes create a new road.
Giggling shadows toss confetti in air,
Life's bright canvas is made to share.

Daring dreams in a whimsical flight,
We chase the laughter until the night.
Every sparkle's just a goofy twist,
In this merry dance, nothing's amiss.

## **Secrets Held in Brilliance**

In comics and snacks, we find our treasure,
But how to explain this secret pleasure?
With chocolate in hand, we giggle and cheer,
As whispers of fudge bring the world near.

Through glimmers of laughter, we dance and sway,
Sharing our secrets in a silly way.
Like finding odd socks in the dryer's doom,
These moments burst forth, filling the room.

## Dreams Painted in Luminescence

A dream of a fish that can ride a bike,
Spinning through barrels, oh what a hike!
We laugh at the thought, a comical sight,
As jellybeans burst in a burst of light.

Unicorns prance with a flair so grand,
While tigers wear shades and take a stand.
They waltz with sunbeams, painting the sky,
In a world so bright, we just can't deny.

## The Pathway of Sunlit Streams

Down by the stream, the frogs wear their hats,
Debating the skills of acrobatic cats.
With splashes of sun and bubbles of cheer,
The fish roll their eyes at our antics here.

As shadows play tricks and twist in delight,
The ducks join the fun, quacking a fright.
Each ripple a laugh, every splash a grin,
We're paddling joy through the chaos within.

## Prism of a Waking World

In morning's embrace, the toaster has dreams,
Of flying toasters with jam-filled schemes.
The coffee pot sings with a jazzy flair,
While crumbs do the cha-cha with nary a care.

The sun peeks through, as if it will tease,
Brightening up all our squeaks and wheeze.
In a symphony of giggles, we trip with glee,
For life's little quirks are the best jubilee.

## Chasing the Deities of Dawn

I woke up late, cup in hand,
My dreams of sunrise, just a band.
Birds chirping loud, what a crew,
I missed my chance, it's nothing new.

Chasing the sun on a Monday spree,
It slipped my mind, it laughed at me.
In pajamas still, I run and joke,
Dawn's light giggles, my sleepy poke.

## A Tapestry of Bright Moments

A riot of colors, socks on the floor,
My cat's bright antics, I can't ignore.
It pounces on shadows, a daring feat,
Each leap a canvas, oh, isn't this sweet?

We paint our days with splashes of fun,
Even when trips to the fridge are a run.
In mismatched hues, we laugh and trip,
Creating a view that's quite a quip.

## Interludes of Brightness

Sunny-side eggs with a comedic twist,
Slipping and sliding, they can't resist.
The toast is a dancer, the butter's a spark,
Breakfast is chaos, let's leave a mark!

Chasing the giggles, they often roam,
In silly hats, we feel at home.
Laughter surrounds us, like sunshine rays,
In our little circus, we dance and play.

## **A Haven of Glowing Hearts**

In a cozy nook, we share bright tales,
A moonlit giggle that never fails.
With marshmallow jokers and cocoa fun,
We toast to the chaos, all buried in sun.

Crafting our dreams with crayons and cheer,
The glow of our laughter attracts all near.
In a blanket fort made of hope and delight,
Everything's silly, and there's no end in sight.

## The Whispering Beacon

A lamp once had a chat with a cat,
Said, 'I shine bright, but what of the bat?'
The cat just giggled, tail in the air,
'You're just a spotlight, with funky flair!'

The shadows danced, put on a show,
While the lamp flickered, 'I'm quite the glow!'
'You're more like a gossip,' the cat did tease,
'Whispering secrets upon the breeze.'

## The Elegance of Soft Beams

A glowbug strutted in fancy attire,
'Behold my elegance, I'm full of fire!'
A moth fluttered past, with disco moves,
'You think you're fancy? Watch how I groove!'

Soft beams chuckled, played peek-a-boo,
'We light up the dance floor, just me and you!'
The insects boogied, feeling quite grand,
'With glimmers and giggles, we'll form a band!'

## A Tapestry of Twinkling Stars


Stars in the sky wore sequined gowns,
Flashing their lights, like cosmic clowns.
'Hey, Big Dipper, you should really twirl!'
I bet you can wow the whole wide world!'

Little stars winked, blushing in fright,
'We're just tiny dots, you're the real light!'
But the moon nudged them, 'No need to pout,
Together we shine, let's rock this bout!'

## Carving Shadows Out of Light

A shadow remarked, 'I'm feeling quite bold,
I paint the world, with stories untold.'
A light replied, 'But I'm the real ace,
Without me, dear friend, you'd vanish without trace!'

They formed a duet, dancing around,
A cartwheel of shapes, sparking joy abound.
'We're partners in crime,' echoed the scene,
'Carving up giggles, bright and serene!'

## Rays of Hope at Dusk

In the sky, colors play,
Dancing shadows in a fray.
A squirrel wearing shades so bright,
Thinks he's famous—what a sight!

As the sun takes a bow,
The clouds form a giggly vow.
Laughing birds dive in delight,
Chasing fireflies, what a flight!

## Illuminated Whispers

Moonlight glimmers on my shoe,
I trip and shout, "What's wrong with you?"
The stars wink with a devilish charm,
While my cat plots a little harm.

I chuckle at shadows on the wall,
They dance around, having a ball.
A ghost appears, but he's out of breath,
He whispers jokes about his death!

## Beneath the Shimmering Veil


Dewdrops sparkle on my toast,
The coffee sings, a morning boast!
Beneath the mist, I start to snicker,
The toaster pops up—what a kicker!

Butterflies wear polka-dot ties,
Sipping nectar, oh my, oh my!
With a wink, they blush a bright hue,
Who knew bugs could dress better too!

## When Daybreak Unfolds

The rooster crows, but it's offbeat,
His rhythm is just not so sweet.
Caffeine rush helps him to strive,
Now he's ready, oh what a drive!

Sunbeams tickle grass so green,
Nature busts out its best routine.
A rabbit hops, then trips in mud,
And we all laugh, what a big thud!

## The Gentle Horizon

A silly rabbit hops so wide,
Chasing rays with silly pride.
He tripped on grass, oh what a sight,
The sun laughed hard, such pure delight.

With every step, a rubber duck,
He squeaks and quacks, oh what bad luck.
The fluffy clouds just roll their eyes,
As shadows dance with cartoon sighs.

## Flashes of Brilliance

A light bulb flicked with sassy flair,
It bounced around without a care.
Like fireflies in a jar of giggles,
Lighting up rooms with funky wiggles.

Each spark is caught in laughter's grip,
With every joke, we twirl and flip.
The punchlines hit like dazzling rays,
In goofy ways, brighten our days.

## The Glint of Unseen Paths

A squirrel in shades skits down a lane,
Its acorn stash is driving it insane.
It trips on branches, avoiding the light,
Making sure it's a comedy bite.

Each glint that shines leads to a jest,
In this nutty chase, it's all in jest.
A golden route, a zigzag gleam,
Life's a funny, wild dream team.

## Through the Canvas of Night

Stars wear hats in a cosmic ball,
They wobble and giggle, taking a fall.
The moon winks with a cheeky glow,
Painting midnight with a funny show.

The owls wear glasses, look very wise,
But trip on branches, oh, such surprise!
They hoot in laughter, not a fright,
In this artwork of a giggly night.

## The Glow of New Beginnings

At dawn, my coffee spills a grin,
It winks at me, I laugh within.
A toast to spills, a floating cheer,
The morning meetings all disappear.

A sock now matched, a feat divine,
It danced alone, a rare design.
A new start giggles, shines so bright,
Even the cat joins in the fight.

Jokes and smiles in a sunny spree,
The calendar's full, come join me!
Each tick and tock, a silly chance,
Life's rhythm calls, so let's all dance.

With silly hats and quirky sights,
We paint the walls with sounds of kites.
A glow ignites from joyful quests,
In this mad world, we are the guests.

## Hues of Enchantment

The jellybeans in rainbow hues,
They laugh and bounce, they sing the blues.
A marvelous mix, a sugary cheer,
In every jar, there's laughter near.

A painted sky, a clown parade,
They drop confetti, a joyful cascade.
Giggles echo as balloons fly high,
A perfect joke, a slice of pie.

The sun wears shades, a cool surprise,
It winks at me with cheery eyes.
To chase the rain with silly grace,
We twirl and spin in a joyful race.

In candy shops, the colors blend,
We feast on laughter, the fun won't end.
Each hue a giggle, each shade a jest,
In this bright world, we are the best.

## A Canvas of Glowing Moments

With crayons bold and paper wide,
We scribble dreams, our hearts collide.
A masterpiece of silly glee,
Each stroke a laugh, come paint with me.

A puddle splashes, shoes gone wild,
I jump right in, like a happy child.
With colors swirling, shining bright,
We chase the sparkles in the night.

An ice cream tower, melting fast,
A sticky giggle, can't make it last.
The drips fall down, a funny flow,
A sweet embrace when we say 'whoa!'

Each moment glows, each laugh we keep,
A treasure chest, our hearts so deep.
The canvas gleams with joy's delight,
In our silly world, we're shining bright.

## Light that Sings

A dance of shadows, the walls sway slow,
The disco ball spins, we steal the show.
Each light bulb flickers, a joyous tune,
Swinging and swaying beneath the moon.

The toaster pops, a bread ballet,
Jam joins in, a fruity fray.
With every crunch, we laugh anew,
Breakfast parties with a joyful crew.

The fridge hums songs of silly bliss,
Each sound a giggle, a funny kiss.
We twirl the spoons, the cups will cheer,
For every note, love's laughter is near.

In this bright realm where fun is king,
We laugh, we jump, we dance and sing.
The world's a stage, no need to fight,
In our laughter's glow, all feels just right.

## Pathways through the Glare

Every time I walk outside,
My sunglasses seem to hide.
I squint and cringe at every beam,
It feels like living in a dream.

The shadows dance, they mock my pace,
As sunbeams try to smirk and chase.
But I just trip on shiny floor,
And laugh about my epic score.

Neighbors stare and point with glee,
'Is that a goat or just a me?'
In routes of gold, I stumble clear,
And show my grace (or lack, I fear).

So here's a tip for anyone keen,
Beware of gleam; it's no routine.
For every ray that fills with cheer,
Just means a tumble's drawing near.

## The Color of Longing

I wander fields of bright, bold hues,
Desiring snacks, but all I choose
Is a buffet of butterflies,
That flit past me with mocking eyes.

I paint my dreams in shades of fun,
A dazzling world under the sun.
But when I reach for bright delight,
I trip and fall, 'tis quite the sight!

The picnic basket's my hot flame,
Yet ants claim mine—it's such a shame.
As sweet snacks vanish, I do groan,
The color of longing—just my own!

So here I sit, with crumbs in hand,
My dreams of treats, not quite as planned.
Yet in this chaos, joy I find,
A colorful banquet of the mind.

## Sunlit Paths in the Wilderness

In the jungle of my daily grind,
I seek for paths that are well-defined.
But every route's a wacky game,
As I lose track and chase my fame.

With branches swinging, leaves at play,
I dance around in a bouncy way.
A squirrel shouts, 'Hey, there's the door!'
But I just trip—oh, there's the floor!

The sunlight sparkles through the trees,
As I chase down the buzzing bees.
My hair's a mess, my shirt's askew,
Yet laughter's found where flowers grew.

These sunny paths that twist and bend,
Are filled with joy; they never end.
Through dappled greens, we prance and leap,
In the wilderness, no time for sleep!

## Dappled Light on Still Waters

Sitting by the pond, I ponder deep,
As ducks swim past and plop, they leap.
Reflections jiggle, dance, and sway,
While I, like them, just wish to play.

A splash erupts—a ripple chase,
I try to stand with perfect grace.
But the mud jumps up to grab my shoe,
And all my friends just laugh anew.

The dappled light, so warm and bright,
Becomes a source of pure delight.
But mischief brews beneath the sheen,
As fish tease me—what do they mean?

In waters still, my thoughts take flight,
Yet chaos reigns, with every bite.
So here I gleam, both wet and wild,
In nature's game, I'm just a child.

## The Play of the Universe's Palette.

In the garden of odd colors bright,
Moonwalking daisies bring pure delight.
Silly squirrels wearing tiny hats,
Throwing acorns like they're baseball bats.

Under cosmic swirls, the comet spins,
Juggling stars like circus twins.
A rainbow slips on a banana peel,
Laughing as it starts to reel.

The sun tickles clouds with golden rays,
While the breeze invents ridiculous ways.
Ticklish flowers giggle and sway,
Inviting all to join the ballet.

Light spills over the grass, such a scene,
Painting shadows that giggle and preen.
The world's a stage, the stars are props,
In this play, happiness never stops.

## Beneath the Glimmering Skies

In a field of fireflies, the dance begins,
As frogs in tuxedos play their violins.
Crickets chirping the night's sweet tune,
While owls wear glasses and act like a loon.

Stars hang like ornaments on a tree,
Sipping on moonlight, so carefree.
The wind shares secrets with bubbling brooks,
As playful ducks write their own story books.

A rainbow stretches, slipping on dew,
Laughs 'til it hiccups, what a view!
The skies giggle, tickling their toes,
While sleepy suns drape over the rows.

Every star winks, a cheeky surprise,
Underneath this magic, joy just flies.
Life's a comedy, stitched with bright threads,
Beneath the glimmering, laughing spreads.

## Shadows Dance in the Radiance

Shadows prance like a playful jest,
Twisting and turning, not letting you rest.
They wear silly hats, jump with glee,
Can you catch them? Not with a cup of tea!

A cat in a top hat leads the parade,
While laughter bubbles in the shade.
Trees sway along to the giggling breeze,
As silly shadows join in with ease.

Bright twinkling stars throw a confetti rain,
As shadows slip in to play the game.
They kick up their heels, do pirouettes,
While the moon chuckles, setting no bets.

At dusk's curtain, laughter twirls and spins,
In this wacky world where fun begins.
Light and shadow in a comical chase,
Holding hands in this radiant space.

## Echoes of Dawn's Embrace

Morning yawns, stretching with flair,
Tips of suns poke everywhere.
A rooster's giggle breaks the hush,
Chasing sleepy clouds in a fluffy rush.

As daisies dance while sipping their tea,
The world hurries to match their glee.
Bees in bow ties zestfully hum,
To the melody that morning's become.

Puppies sniffing at every tree,
Wondering what snack could possibly be.
The echo of laughter rolls like a wave,
In the dawn's embrace, nothing misbehaves.

Rays of sunlight skip on the ground,
With every giggle, joy can be found.
In this hour so bright and sweet,
A funny world, where hearts skip a beat.

## Shadows Dance at Dusk

In the corner, I saw him trip,
He thought he'd glide, but took a dip.
The shadows laughed, their wiggle free,
As he got up, 'Was that for me?'

The trees began their nightly twirl,
Leaves swirling round in a playful whirl.
I joined the jig with a silly stance,
Two left feet, caught in the dance!

The moon winked down, a glowing clown,
As crickets chirped their silly sound.
A raccoon peeked from the bushes near,
With a wink, he joined the evening cheer.

The stars appeared, all in a row,
As if to say, 'Enjoy the show!'
So we twirled and spun in the dark,
Echoing laughter, a joyful spark.

## Reflections of Dawn

The morning sun, it stretched and yawned,
While sleepy flowers dew-drenched pawned.
I saw a bee in a sleepy flight,
Buzzing loud, 'I'm late! Oh, what a fright!'

The coffee pot began to sing,
'Wake up, humans! It's time for bling!'
I danced with toast, a pop-up round,
It landed butter-side up, and I frowned.

A squirrel leaped with a nut so wide,
'Finders keepers!' He scoffed with pride.
But tripped on a branch, tumbled around,
He rolled and then... could not be found!

Sunbeam rays started to play,
Chasing shadows that ran away.
With giggles waking up the town,
The day began with laughter's crown.

## In the Glow of Quiet Moments

A cozy nook with fuzzy socks,
My cat plots schemes with sly little knocks.
She leaps for the lamp like it's a mouse,
Then scared of her shadow, hides in the house.

Tea was brewing, a fragrant bliss,
I spilled a bit, and oh, what a mess!
The mug wobbled on the edge of fate,
'Time to mop up!' I exclaimed, feeling late.

Then came a knock, my friend in sight,
With mismatched socks, all colorful and bright.
We laughed at the chaos, spilled some more,
Creating memories that we adore.

The glow of moments passed like steam,
Where little things ignite big dreams.
With laughter bubbling in the air,
The quiet moments danced with flair.

## **Embracing the Daybreak**

The rooster crowed, but missed the cue,
Caught in a laugh, he sang out of tune.
The sun peeked over, a golden face,
Yelling, 'Rise up! It's time to race!'

I stepped outside with sleepy hair,
A broom became a sword, I swore to dare.
'Fight the dust bunnies!' I declared with glee,
While neighbors giggled at my warrior spree.

The wind blew soft with a teasing nudge,
As if to say, 'Don't hold that grudge.'
I took a leap, in a froggy hop,
And plopped on the grass with a giggle and flop!

Daybreak dawned in a vibrant hue,
Each blade of grass sparkled with dew.
We embraced joy in every little way,
Welcoming fun in the light of day.

## Whispers of a Sunlit Future

In the morning, my coffee spills,
A dance of beans, it gives me chills.
I laugh at chaos, a cheerful mess,
As sunlight beams, I feel so blessed.

Cat on the windowsill, wide awake,
Stares at shadows, jumps with a quake.
Chasing dust mites like tiny spies,
With moonlit dreams in her clever eyes.

Jelly on toast, a sticky fight,
My breakfast wiggles, oh what a sight.
The butter slips like a comical show,
With each big bite, I can't help but glow.

Laughter echoes when I trip and fall,
Sunshine giggles behind the wall.
Even with bruises, I wear a grin,
For the day is bright, let the fun begin!

## **Glowing Trails of Destiny**

On a path made of sparkles and gleam,
I run with joy, a candy dream.
A squirrel wearing shades, oh so cool,
Steals my sandwich, that little fool.

In the park, a dog spins like a top,
Chasing his tail, he just won't stop.
And I laugh out loud at his funny dance,
Under the rays, I take my chance.

Bubbles float high in the warm blue air,
Popped by giggles, they vanish with flair.
The sun kisses grass, it laughs too tight,
All in pursuit of pure delight.

Chasing a kite that flies with grace,
I stumble and trip, oh what a race!
But in the glow of this sunny spree,
Life's just a joke, come laugh with me!

## The Light's Gentle Caress

Waking up late, sunshine's a tease,
Pajamas still on, oh, what a breeze.
The world outside giggles as I yawn,
In this warm glow, my cares are gone.

Grass tickles my toes as I run around,
With the dog rolling, we both hit the ground.
A game of chase, he outsmarts the sun,
In this funny race, it's all in good fun.

Faces at picnics share silly grins,
With lemonade spills and cheeky sins.
The ants hold parties under a tree,
While I sip juice and just roam free.

Slipping on slides, a playground delight,
In the bright world, everything's right.
With each bright chuckle, the day's a win,
Let's frolic till sundown, come join in!

## In the Embrace of Glimmers

Twinkling stars in the clumsy night,
Pinatas burst in a comical sight.
We gather the candy, all loose and wild,
With giggles and chuckles, we're all just a child.

Chasing moonbeams that dance on the floor,
Our feet make echoes, we want to explore.
The glow of the night, a merry parade,
In this silly warmth, all worries fade.

A toad sings opera, such a loud croak,
While friends burst out laughing at every joke.
Under the twinkle of a silver glow,
Together we make the best kind of show.

As dawn approaches, we all are one,
In this silly dream where we laugh and run.
So let's take these moments, full of cheer,
In the embrace of glimmers, we have no fear!

## **In the Glow of Tender Moments**

In the waltz of the late-night snacks,
My cat sneezes, and the popcorn clacks.
A dance of crumbs on the floor so bright,
Who knew a snack could lead to a fight?

The fridge hums softly, a tune so sweet,
I tiptoe to raid it, a midnight treat.
But my sock gets caught, oh what a plight,
I'm stuck in the kitchen, a comical sight!

With a spoon in one hand and a bowl in the other,
I mimic a chef, but I'm not any better.
A tangle of noodles and salad gone wrong,
The neighbors must think I'm composing a song!

Yet in the chaos, I laugh with delight,
For tender moments make life feel so bright.
In this silly banquet—a comedic spree,
I find joy in the mess, oh so carefree!

## The Luminous Horizon

The sun spoke softly, a cheeky grin,
Said, "Let's brighten the world, let the fun begin!"
Clouds wore shades, how stylish they seemed,
As they plotted silly pranks while I dreamed.

A cat on a roof, with the coolest of hats,
Critiques my attire, oh how he chats!
"Your sunglasses are out, dear human, I swear,
Why not borrow these wings if you care?"

Birds stage a concert, a chirping delight,
Strutting their feathers, they put on a fright.
With each note they sing, my giggles erupt,
It's a laughter-filled world that can't be corrupted.

In this luminous glow, mischief does play,
As laughter dances in a kooky ballet.
The horizon sparkles, with hilarity rife,
And I can't help but love this fun-loving life!

## Beneath the Gilded Canopy

Under the branches where shadows arrive,
I spotted a squirrel, oh my, what a dive!
He fancied his chance to snag a loose nut,
But tripped on a branch and fell on his butt!

The leaves overhead chuckled, swaying with glee,
As I guffawed loudly, what a sight to see!
Even the sunbeams took up the jest,
A cozy tableau, nature at its best.

With twigs and acorns crafting a crown,
I crowned myself king, though I wore just a frown.
The bugs held a court, all buzzing with pride,
Yet my royal decree was a playful slide!

Beneath this canopy, laughter can bloom,
As the world spins on, chasing away gloom.
In this gilded retreat, humor's our guide,
Creating sweet moments we can't let slide!

## Flickers in the Twilight

In the twilight's embrace, the fireflies dance,
Their glowing behinds set a whimsical trance.
I tried to catch one, but it slipped right away,
"Hey, come back here!" I laughed, what a display.

A raccoon peeked in, with a curious peek,
He'd hoped for a snack, but I gave a shriek.
In this funny patch of squabbles and cheer,
Twilight giggles whispered, "We're all welcome here!"

With shadows as friends, the night can surprise,
A comedy playground beneath starlit skies.
The moon chuckles softly, twinkling above,
As our spirits flicker, wrapped up in love.

So here's to the laughter that glows in the night,
In the stillness of dusk, everything feels right.
As each silly moment breaks through with a spark,
We create tales of joy, igniting the dark!

**Pulse of the Glimmering Night**

The moon wears shades of lavender,
Stars play hopscotch on the breeze,
Owls gossip about the daylight,
While crickets laugh with ease.

A raccoon steals a shiny spoon,
Dancing like he's at a ball,
The night gets tipsy on a tune,
Echoing underneath it all.

Fireflies hold a lantern race,
Buzzing jokes with zest and cheer,
Each flicker lights a silly face,
Their giggles we can almost hear.

The moon winks down with mischief bright,
A nighttime game of tag unfolds,
With shadows soft and hearts so light,
It's laughter that the evening holds.

## The Gentle Brush of Radiant Tides

Waves whisper secrets to the shore,
While seaweed wigs wave back in glee,
A crab in disco shoes galore,
Struts like it's a jubilee.

Seagulls play cards with the breeze,
Trading stories of the day,
One bird wins a golden cheese,
While the others cheer and sway.

The sand tickles toes that dance,
As sunbeams join the crazy flight,
In this sun-kissed, happy trance,
Both day and night get quite the fright.

A dolphin jumps, a belly flop,
Splashing laughter in the air,
While kids just can't seem to stop,
Building castles everywhere.

## **Dawn's Promise in the Gloaming**

Morning yawns and stretches wide,
Pancakes flip in the brightening sky,
Squirrels trade their sleepy pride,
While birds rehearse a song to try.

A snoozy cat wakes with a pout,
Tipping over from its dream,
While coffee brews amidst the clout,
The sun spills light like whipped cream.

Breezes blow a playful tune,
Tickling noses with a wink,
Daffodils do a morning swoon,
Turning petals to the pink.

As laughter bubbles like a stream,
Dawn invites us to play along,
With whispers of a happy dream,
It's time to join the joyful throng.

## Fragments Underneath the Celestial Glow

A comet spins in silly dance,
While planets giggle in delight,
Twinkle, twinkle, take a chance,
To join this cosmic pillow fight.

Galaxies weave a patchwork night,
Tangled in a quilt of shines,
Each star a wink, a bit of light,
Trading secrets with their signs.

Asteroids throw confetti bright,
Celebrating all their orbits,
Catch them all, hold on so tight,
As they play beneath the limits.

The universe hums its funny song,
While comets race against the time,
In this grand adventure, we belong,
Laughing through the stellar rhyme.

## Glimmers of Forgotten Dreams

In the attic, dust bunnies roam,
Old toys whisper, 'Take me home!'
A sock puppet sneezes with glee,
While the clock ticks on, tea time's spree.

A jester's hat on a photo frame,
Old gossip's left of a wilting flame.
Marbles roll like secret agents,
Under the bed lies hidden patience.

A teddy bear pulls a cheeky grin,
Hiding secrets of thick and thin.
A dream catcher tangled in twine,
Collects all giggles, turns them into wine.

So come with a smile and a dance,
In this attic of odd happenstance.
Let's toast to dreams that never did call,
In the shadows, we find joy after all.

## The Celestial Pathway

Stars wear hats made of glowing cheese,
While comets zip by with a gentle tease.
With space squirrels, we launch into flight,
Chasing moonbeams, oh what a sight!

Asteroids bounce like rubber balls,
And in this void, laughter calls.
Riding on rings of Saturn so round,
With each giggle, we spin, we bound.

Aliens dance in a hula-hoop,
Juggling planets with a merry whoop.
In zero gravity, we tumble and glide,
No worries to tether, just joy for the ride.

So step right up to this cosmic show,
Where each twinkle gives a happy glow.
Join the parade, let the laughter ignite,
On this whimsical journey through the night.

## Soft Hues of the Evening

As the sun blushes a drowsy mint,
Chickens argue, giving the hint.
The sky's palette splashes a wink,
While crickets challenge the day's last drink.

Clouds don pajamas, cozy and fluffy,
As sleepy heads find their days get stuffy.
The garden gnome takes a stretch and yawn,
Declaring himself the king of dawn.

Fireflies flicker with fancy flair,
While the moon rolls in, a debonair.
A breeze brings whispers, sweet and bright,
Of silly antics through the night.

So gather 'round, dear friends, a delight,
In these hues where dreams take flight.
The night giggles with whimsy and cheer,
As we toast to laughter, loud and clear.

## The Radiant Crossing

At the crossing, where shadows play,
Socks mate at noon, a bright ballet.
With umbrellas twirling like butterflies,
Who knew weather could come in such a guise?

The pavement smiles at our clumsy feet,
As taxis honk with a jazzy beat.
Pigeons show off their best backflips,
While ice cream drips from delighted lips.

A street performer juggles with flair,
Throwing apples high, 'It's magic, I swear!'
A kid bursts forth with a leap and bound,
Claiming the world is a playground, profound.

So let's skip through this lively parade,
Where each footstep creates a cascade.
In this radiant moment, carefree and true,
Life's just fun, and you're invited too!

## **Flickers of a Forgotten World**

In shadows cast by clumsy feet,
The gnomes play chess with mops and sheep.
A pickle jar sings a silly tune,
While sunbeams dance with a lazy broom.

Dust bunnies roll like tumbleweeds,
In the corners, they plot their misdeeds.
A cat with style, in sunglasses pried,
Claims the throne where chaos resides.

The clock ticks back, or is that a joke?
Time's on vacation, it's breaking the yolk.
Jelly beans wear top hats in flair,
In this world of whims, nothing's quite fair.

So laugh with the gnomes, sing with the sun,
Join the pickle jar—oh, what fun!
It's a flicker of laughter, a wink to the night,
In the corners of dreams, everything's right.

## The Glorious Awakening

Woke up to a toast with legs, it struts,
Marmalade dancing, oh how it cuts!
A cereal box speaks in riddles bright,
Claiming it won last year's food fight.

The curtains giggle, they flap about,
While rugs do the cha-cha, there's no doubt.
A bedbug diva takes center stage,
In this morning circus, we feel no rage.

The sun peeks in with a cheeky grin,
Inviting all to join in the spin.
Lemonade flows like a chorus of bees,
Leaves twerking gently in the soft breeze.

So grab your toast, wear your best smile,
The glorious morn calls for a wild style.
As laughter awakens the sleepy-eyed,
Join this dance, let sweet joy be our guide.

# Through the Keyhole of Day

A squirrel in a suit spins a tale,
Of acorns that sailed on a peppermint gale.
Sunlight whispers secrets to the walls,
Tickling the moths, making them fall.

Jellyfish drummers beat their strange tune,
While butterflies wear capes in bright hues.
A raccoon poet scribbles in chalk,
Sketching the dreams that moonbeams talk.

The breakfast plates polish their chatter,
As forks dive in for a giggling platter.
A toast with the sun, a wink from the moon,
Kick-starts the day with a vibrant tune.

Through the keyhole where whimsy shines,
Each corner giggles, each moment twines.
In this playful world, anything is fair,
Just open your heart and dance with the air.

## Carnivals of Shimmering Reflections

In the mirror, a clown gives a wink,
Juggling marshmallows, it makes you think.
Cotton candy clouds fluff up the sky,
As elephants stomp and the gummy bears fly.

A tightrope walker made of spaghetti,
Twirls on onions—oh, what a Betty!
The popcorn pops with a laugh and a leap,
While licorice snakes in a line so deep.

Balloons have started a silly parade,
With jokes written on every shade.
The lemonade fountain splashes delight,
As friends hold hands in the fading light.

These carnivals twinkle with fun galore,
Each quirky moment, never a bore.
So step right up, let laughter enthrall,
In this shimmering mirror, we party for all!

## Embers of Hope's Rise

In the ashes of burnt toast,
I find my treasure lost,
Crispy edges, golden hopes,
A breakfast worth its cost.

The coffee brews like Friday night,
A dance of beans and steam,
My mug's a trophy, oh so bright,
Winner of the morning theme.

Eggs juggling on the pan,
A circus act in my kitchen,
Yolk bursts out like an eager fan,
Who knew my brunch would be glitchin'?

As sunlight sneaks through the blinds,
I laugh at my sleepy face,
With every chuckle, joy unwinds,
In this cozy, silly space.

## The Glittering Edge of Dreams

In dreamland where the socks unite,
All mismatched pairs feel just right,
They dance and spin, oh what a sight,
Whispering softly, 'Sock fight tonight!'

The pillows form a giant throne,
Where I am king, the queen's my phone,
Ruling over lands of foam,
In this kingdom made of home.

Chasing shadows of my snack,
A cookie monster on a track,
With crumbs that point the way, no lack,
The chocolate calls; I can't turn back!

I wake to find my crown is toast,
A piece gone missing, oh the roast,
Yet with a giggle, I can boast,
My dreams were wild; they matter most.

## Painting the Day with Light

With colors splashed like morning cheer,
I paint the sky, I twirl, I steer,
Blue for calm, then yellow near,
Oops, my cat has now appeared!

She leaps and lands amid the hues,
Her paws a mix of vibrant blues,
A masterpiece, my muse, it's true,
As she creates her own reviews.

The sun spills out its golden rays,
Mixes with my clumsy ways,
As I spark joy on cloudy days,
A canvas bright, where laughter plays.

With every stroke, my heart takes flight,
In splattered paint, there's pure delight,
In this messy art, I find my light,
Life's silly scenes, I'll hold them tight.

## Soft Glows of Yesterday

Memories flicker like old film rolls,
Playground laughter, and silly shoals,
Chasing ice cream trucks, our hungry souls,
Dancing in dirt, we were rock and rolls.

Those afternoons, with endless sun,
Where adults seemed like they had fun,
Stuck in time, we'd all outrun,
A world of dreams just begun.

Funny hats on our heads so grand,
A parade of kids, hand in hand,
Every mishap, a comic stand,
Life's a joke, we all understand.

As the soft glow dims, I take a breath,
Finding joy in the echoes left,
For laughter, my heart's true wealth,
In yesterday's tales, I've found my stealth.

## Moments of Warmth and Wonder

In a room filled with laughter,
A cat tries to catch a ray,
She leaps and tumbles with grace,
But oh, the light slips away!

Uncles dance with funny hats,
Spinning tales of days gone by,
A toast to the silliest quirks,
As the sun waves from the sky.

Grandma's cookies, warm and sweet,
Seem to chatter, oh so bright,
While smiles melt the coldest heart,
In this cozy afternoon light.

With every giggle, joy ignites,
Creating moments, soft and rare,
In this little world we've built,
Where every beam is a friendly stare.

## When Shadows Break

In a park where shadows play,
A dog thinks he can fly,
He leaps for frisbees, quite confused,
And lands with a goofy sigh.

Children giggle, shadows bounce,
As they run beneath the trees,
Twisting like pretzels in the breeze,
Yelling 'Catch that sunbeams' please!'

A squirrel steals a sandwich slice,
While birds chirp a silly tune,
As the clock tickles our senses,
Dancing light brings joy, not gloom.

With every shadow stretching long,
The world feels brighter than before,
As laughter echoes, joy ignites,
And we spill secrets on the floor.

# A Symphony of Soft Light

In the kitchen, pots do sing,
While the blender spins a tune,
With flour flying high and low,
A powdered chef is born by noon.

The toaster pops, with such a flair,
Like fireworks that cheer and shout,
Bread dances forth, a golden show,
While out the window, sunbeams spout.

A curtain flutters, in a breeze,
Twirling like a ballerina bright,
While spoons conduct the sunny rays,
Composing dreams in frosted light.

Each moment shines as laughter swells,
And the day hums a happy beat,
In this world of radiant joy,
Where even chores can feel so sweet.

**Luminescent Journeys**

On a bike ride through the park,
A squirrel shouts, 'I'll race you now!'
With hurried paws and silly hops,
And the bright sun witnessing our vow.

The pond reflects a million giggles,
As ducks quack out a playful tune,
They splash around like silly fools,
Creating ripples in the afternoon.

We chase each other under trees,
With dappled sunlight painting the ground,
And every twist and every turn,
Finds us laughing, joyfully unbound.

With every pedal, hearts take flight,
In this whimsical, bright domain,
Where every ride brings glowing tales,
And silly moments will remain.

**Singing with the Morning Rays**

Oh, the sun peeks, what a sight,
Stirring coffee with pure delight.
Birds chirp tunes, quite a show,
And my cat attempts to flow.

Pancakes flipping, syrup's a dance,
Spilled all over—now that's my chance!
With butter melting, golden glee,
Who knew breakfast held comedy?

Socks mismatched, hair all a frizz,
Mirror reflects—a bright fizz quiz.
A dance party starts, just me and my mug,
Stepping on toes—oh, what a shrug!

As the rays stretch, laughter erupts,
Chasing shadows, the world constructs.
Join the singing, don't delay,
Morning antics lead the way!

## In the Realm of Gentle Brightness


In a garden of glow, I stumble and trip,
Chasing butterflies, I lose my grip.
Petunias giggle, what a tease,
As I step on daisies with utmost ease.

Sunbeams tickling, what a blast,
While ants throw parties, growing fast.
They invite me, I bring the bread,
Oops! My sandwich is a worm's spread!

Glimmers dancing on leaves so green,
While squirrels debate the best cuisine.
Bees taking orders, oh what a fuss,
'I'll have a nectar latte, no wait for us!'

In this realm where chuckles sprout,
Even shadows wear a joyful clout.
With giggles echoing, dance we must,
In brightness gentle, we find our trust!

## The Solstice of Heartbeats

As calendars twist with glowing zeal,
My heart does a jig and forgets to heel.
Counting moments like a pie in the sky,
Every tick-tock bids the time goodbye.

The sun throws a party, shining so bright,
While clouds crash in, turning day into night.
But fear not, for stars bring their flair,
Whispering jokes that float in the air.

In the garden, laughter grows like trees,
Tickled by breezes, dancing with ease.
Each heartbeat a drum, no need to be shy,
As we twirl and spin, it's the only way to fly!

So here we are, in this playful trance,
With each rising sun, we happen to dance.
The solstice sings a rhythm so sweet,
With funny little heartbeats, life's a treat!

## A Carousel of Colors

Round and round the hues do spin,
A pink giraffe with a cheeky grin.
Blue elephants dance in the sun,
While yellow zebras are just for fun.

The purple cow mooed out a tune,
As green balloons floated like a balloon.
Orange rabbits hop with glee,
Painting rainbows for you and me.

With each whirl, laughter takes flight,
Chasing giggles into the night.
Splashing colors, oh what a sight,
On this carousel, we feel just right.

## Chasing Shadows of the Past

Once a ghost wore a top hat bright,
Danced with shadows, what a sight!
He tripped on his cape, fell on the ground,
All the whispers, oh what a sound!

With every step, shadows would sway,
Bumping into walls, they'd play all day.
A shadow cat brought a fishy snack,
Only to find it rolling back!

Echoes of laughter fill the air,
As swirling fog twirls without a care.
Snatching moments with great delight,
Chasing shadows into the night.

## Threads of Illumination

A loom of giggles spins so bright,
With threads of humor, pure delight.
Woven tales of quirky dreams,
In every stitch, laughter streams.

Patchwork suns and moonlit glee,
Stitching smiles for you and me.
Knots of joy in every seam,
Making life a vibrant theme.

With every tug, the colors play,
Pulling at hearts in a funny way.
Threads of sunlight, dance and twirl,
In this tapestry, life's a whirl.

## Spectrum of Solitude

In quiet corners, quirks delight,
Peculiar ducks in hats so bright.
A penguin sips a cup of tea,
While a shy tortoise tells a spree.

Dancing alone in a streak of cheer,
Silly antics that bring us near.
Laughing with socks and mismatched shoes,
Creating fun in solitude's hues.

When silence sings, the spirits rise,
Finding solace 'neath laugh-filled skies.
In solitude, the humor's grand,
A spectrum painted by our own hand.

## Flickers of the Rising Star

In the kitchen, pots all clang,
The cat jumps high, then does a twang.
Bacon sizzles, pancakes flip,
But I just spilled a whole cup—drip!

The toaster shoots my toast like darts,
It lands right in my neighbor's arts.
With coffee brewed like rocket fuel,
I ponder if I went to school.

The sun peeks through my window bright,
And chases shadows, what a sight!
I dance around, all limbs a-flail,
And wonder if I might prevail.

## Illuminated by the Moon's Embrace

The moonlight shines on my pet turtle,
He thinks he's fast, but he's just hurtled.
As I sneak snacks, he gives a stare,
I swear he thinks he runs the lair.

With lopsided shadows all around,
I trip on things that make no sound.
A nearby owl hoots, gives me looks,
Like I got lost between the books.

Under the stars, my laughter rings,
While searching for my missing things.
I blame the wind for all my woes,
Yet here I am, striking silly poses.

## **Radiant Fragments of Time**

In the garden, weeds have taken flight,
I chase them down, they put up a fight.
A butterfly mocks my clumsy run,
I fall face-first, and that's no fun!

Clock ticks loudly, time's not my friend,
I swear it bends, this makes no end.
Daisies giggle as I pull out grass,
They seem to know that I won't pass.

A clockwork squirrel steals my snack,
I toss a nut, but it won't hack.
Time's a jester, antics are wild,
And I'm just here, a goofy child.

## The Edge of Hazy Horizons

On the horizon, clouds take a dive,
The wind's so strong, it makes me jive.
I trip over dreams that float on by,
While pancake plans just wave goodbye.

My kite is stuck in a neighbor's tree,
I wave at squirrels, they stare at me.
I wonder if they think I'm weird,
Yet here I am, completely cheered.

The horizon blushes, a sunset mess,
While I munch treats and find my dress.
With giggles echoing in the air,
I toss my worries, without a care.

## Whispers of Radiance

In the nook, a shadow danced,
It tripped on air, and quite advanced.
A giggle slipped from lamp's bright glow,
Said, "Watch your step, it's quite a show!"

The cat misjudged its sunny spot,
Landed flat, and looked distraught.
"It's rather bright, my furry friend!"
"You've found my rays, let's pretend!"

Mice form lines in slick parade,
With cheese on wheels, their plans are laid.
They squeak and squeal, they swirl and twirl,
In this corner, chaos will unfurl!

So when you see the sunlight peek,
Just know there's mischief on the streak.
For laughter lingers, warm and bright,
In every corner, growing light.

## Silhouettes Beneath the Sun

Beneath the rays, a shadow croaked,
A little bird that giggled and poked.
It tried to sing but missed the note,
Instead, it chirped like a tiny goat.

A dog lay sprawled, dreaming of meat,
Chasing shadows with its little feet.
"Fetch that sunbeam!" the kids all cried,
And laughed as he rolled with all his pride.

Two squirrels raced—a comical sight,
Dodging shadows with all their might.
One tripped and fell on his fluffy tail,
"Next time, let's stick to the trail!"

In this fun dance of light and shade,
Each giggle weaves a bright charade.
For in the sun, the antics play,
And laughter glimmers through the day.

# The Lullaby of the Evening

As twilight creeps on little feet,
The moonlight hums a tune so sweet.
Stars start to giggle in the night,
"Did we just win this radiant fight?"

A cricket chirps with all its might,
Confidently, it calls the night.
"Hey firefly, don't blink too fast,
Or you'll just fade, our fun won't last!"

Beneath the glow, a moth took flight,
Enthralled by dreams of silly light.
With loops and swirls, it spun around,
Until it landed on the ground!

So let's all sing this silvery song,
Where laughter twinkles and hearts belong.
In this lullaby, let joy take wing,
The evening glows, and we all sing!

## Echoes in a Sunbeam

A dandelion, fluffy and bold,
Dreamed of places, brash and old.
"Watch out, world! Here I come!"
But the breeze just laughed, "You're such fun!"

A sunbeam tickled a garden gnome,
"Stop grinning like you've found a home!"
But gnome just shrugged, "It's not so bad,
Especially when I'm feeling glad!"

Ants on a march, with crumbs in tow,
Bumble along in a gleeful row.
When one trips over, they all proclaim,
"Next time, stick to the... lively game!"

With each wink of sun's playful stroke,
The day breaks out in laughter's cloak.
For in these echoes of golden light,
The world is funny, oh what a sight!

## **Where Radiance Beckons**

In the glow of a sunny day,
Napping cats chase beams of play.
My coffee spills with cheeky glee,
As shadows dance and laugh with me.

The fridge hums like a rockstar bold,
While leftovers tell tales of old.
The floor creaks under my swirling feet,
As socks conspire to claim defeat.

A lightbulb flickers, starts a game,
Of hide-and-seek, it's quite the fame.
The toaster pops, and crumbs take flight,
In this cozy chaos, all feels right.

So here we bask in rays absurd,
With giggles echoing, sweetly heard.
Life's silly moments are a delight,
In the brilliance of every light.

## Illuminated Memories

There's a candle that thinks it's a star,
Wishing to shine near and far.
A dance-off with a dusty broom,
As laughter echoes through the room.

Grandma's stories take joyful flight,
Of socks mis-matched in morning light.
With each retelling, her eyes would twinkle,
Like fairy lights that softly crinkle.

Mom's pineapple upside-down cake,
A dessert that makes our mouths ache.
It slips off the plate, a comical blob,
And serves us all a laughter sob.

With friends who turn the mundane bright,
We sip lemonade till the fall of night.
Each moment glowing in our hearts,
Where funny tales and love imparts.

## An Odyssey of Light

Adventures beckon from the sun,
With jokes exchanged and hugs all done.
A squirrel steals fries, a daring heist,
In this light-hearted, vibrant feast.

The dog wears shades, looking so cool,
While kids flip flips by the pool.
A beach ball's fate, a wild drifter,
As laughter flies, the sun shines brighter.

Flip-flops squeak in the goofiest way,
As sand gets stuck, it tries to stay.
We chase the sun, with spirits soaring,
Creating memories, forever pouring.

With every sunset, the giggles grow,
In twilight's glow, our hearts all know.
These moments shine like a starry night,
In an odyssey filled with pure delight.

**Flickering Dreams and Wishes**

The firefly winks, a flirty tease,
As we make wishes with playful ease.
Under the stars, we giggle and sigh,
While marshmallows roast as fireflies fly.

A raccoon peeks through the picnic spread,
Stealing crumbs while we laugh instead.
"Hey, buddy, share!" we shout with glee,
As the sneaky bandit scampers free.

Summer night, with dreams on the rise,
Catching laughs that light up the skies.
In every flicker, a funny plight,
With wishes whispered into the night.

So let's embrace this joyous spree,
With dreams and laughter, wild and free.
For in these moments, we find our bliss,
Under the stars, we steal a kiss.

## The Warmth of Silent Radiance

In a room, the sunbeams dance,
Tickling cats, they take a chance.
Socks are warmed on the floor's embrace,
As dust bunnies make their quiet race.

A toaster pops, it starts to sing,
Toasty bread, oh what joy it brings!
The light displays its funny flair,
Makes all the shadows unaware.

Dishes sparkle in a playful show,
As the dishwasher hums a friendly row.
Watch the spoons, how they do sway,
In the glow of a sunny day.

Lampshades giggle, twinkle, and glow,
Casting shadows that twist and flow.
In every nook, a joke unfolds,
By the warmth, the heart consoled.

## Caresses from the Celestial

Stars wink down with cheeky grace,
Lighting up the dark's embrace.
A moonbeam's tickle on your nose,
Makes you giggle, who knows?

Planets spin in a comedy spin,
While comets race with a cheeky grin.
Galaxies swirl like a cosmic dance,
In this universe, we take a chance.

Venus teases Mars, oh what a fray,
Tugging at hearts in a playful way.
Orbits laugh, they twist and twirl,
Celestial pranks, a cosmic whirl.

With every dawn, the laughter grows,
Painting skies in radiant flows.
The sun spills coffee on the earth,
While the clouds chuckle at our mirth.

## **Threads of Illumination**

A spider spins lights from the sun,
Creating webs, oh what fun!
Each dew drop catches a bright beam,
Making every corner gleam.

Fairies giggle, they tiptoe near,
With sparkles that twinkle like some crazy cheer.
Fairy dust flies during tea time,
Inviting all to laugh and rhyme.

Sunshine threads through leaves so bright,
Making every bug feel light.
A squirrel plays tag with a ray,
As shadows jump and sway.

Butterflies join in the frolic spree,
Winking at the flowers with glee.
In the garden, it's a funny fête,
As laughter blooms and won't abate.

## **In the Embrace of Serenity**

Beneath the tree, a nap we take,
While dreams and squirrels swirl and quake.
A breeze slips through, oh what a tease,
As dandelions bob with ease.

Rabbits play hopscotch on the lane,
Doing flips in the gentle rain.
Each puddle forms a new surprise,
As giggles echo to the skies.

Tea sets welcome ants in a row,
Who sip the drops like they're in a show.
The sunlight spills, a golden throw,
As bees dance 'round, swaying to and fro.

Every moment filled with cheer,
Nature's laughter linger near.
In quiet corners, joy won't cease,
In the soft light, we find our peace.

## Caress of a Golden Hour

Sunbeams dance on my nose,
Tickling my thoughts like a rose.
I laugh at the shadows, they giggle too,
As they stretch and yawn, enjoying the view.

Chasing my dog, who leaps with flair,
He thinks he's the king, with his prideful air.
A squirrel mocks us from up in a tree,
"Catch if you can!" it cries with glee.

The ice cream truck jingles down the street,
My taste buds burst with sugary heat.
But dad just says, "Just one scoop, please!"
I roll my eyes while he aims to tease.

Sunset paints the sky, a woeful sight,
But tomorrow brings laughter, it's always bright.
For every giggle in this warm ray's shine,
Makes life a banquet, truly divine.

## A Tapestry of Sunlit Dreams

Pillow fights with cotton clouds,
Laughing out loud, banishing shrouds.
Jumping on beds, a homebound flight,
Safety nets of joy, such a delight!

The trees whisper secrets, oh so sweet,
As I try to dance with my two left feet.
Spilled lemonade becomes a stage,
In this sunlit script, we write our age.

Chasing shadows with giggles so bright,
Even the moon hums a tune at night.
Dreams become wild in warm golden beams,
As we laugh in the fabric of our dreams.

In sunlit patches, we weave our play,
Each chuckle's a bead, brightening the day.
Life's tapestry's woven with threads so bold,
And each little laugh is worth more than gold.

## Glimmers of Hope in the Dark

In the night, I search for glares,
While my cat stalks my unkempt hair.
She pounces softly, does her best,
While I squeak out a startled jest!

The fridge hums loudly, a song so bright,
Chasing my fears away in the night.
"What's there to eat?" a grumbling rhyme,
While I seek snacks to pass the time.

Every creak in the shadows plays tricks,
Making me fumble for any mix.
"Is it a ghost, or just my sock?"
Maybe it's just my dinner clock!

A glimmer of hope in cookie dough,
As I bake my way to a sweetened glow.
Laughter bubbles up, a warm embrace,
Where even the dark has a funnier face.

## The Soft Touch of Twilight

Twilight whispers, a gentle wink,
As fireflies gather, making me think.
"Are we late for the party?" they joke and prance,
In this soft twilight, all creatures dance.

Grills are roaring with a savory cheer,
While I search for burgers—oh, they disappear!
"Who stole my bun?" I dramatically cry,
As my brother chuckles, with a mouthful nearby.

The sky melts slowly in shades of pink,
Cats lounge on fences, just starting to think.
As the sun sneaks away, hiding its face,
We gather for stories in the twilight's embrace.

With laughter as bright as the stars above,
This soft touch of evening wraps us in love.
For every chuckle beneath the dark dome,
Means nights like these feel perfectly home.

www.ingramcontent.com/pod-product-compliance
Lightning Source LLC
Chambersburg PA
CBHW070305120526
44590CB00017B/2572